THE PORT OF NEW YORK

Bird's-Eye View from the Battery, Looking South | Currier & I

STATEN ISLAND

NEW JERSEY

ROBBINS REEF LIGHTHOUSE

Kate's Light

KATE WALKER AT ROBBINS REEF LIGHTHOUSE

Elizabeth Spires

ILLUSTRATED BY

Emily Arnold McCully

MARGARET FERGUSON BOOKS
HOLIDAY HOUSE · NEW YORK

For Jane Gelfman and Deborah Schneider—E.S.

The publisher wishes to thank Megan Beck,
curator at The Noble Maritime Collection,
for her expert review of the text.

Margaret Ferguson Books
Text copyright © 2021 by Elizabeth Spires
Illustrations copyright © 2021 by Emily Arnold McCully
All Rights Reserved
HOLIDAY HOUSE is registered in the U.S. Patent and Trademark Office.
Printed and bound in September 2020 at Leo Paper, Heshan, China.
The artwork was created with watercolor and pen and ink.
www.holidayhouse.com
First Edition
1 3 5 7 9 10 8 6 4 2

Library of Congress Cataloging-in-Publication Data

Names: Spires, Elizabeth, author. | McCully, Emily Arnold, illustrator.
Title: Kate's Light : Kate Walker at Robbins Reef Lighthouse
Elizabeth Spires ; illustrations by Emily Arnold McCully,
Other titles: Kate Walker at Robbins Reef Lighthouse
Description: First edition. | New York : Holiday House, [2021]
Includes bibliographical references. | Audience: Ages 6-8 | Audience: Grades 2-3
Summary: "A biography of Kate Walker, one of the first women on the Eastern
seaboard to be put in charge of an offshore lighthouse."—Provided by publisher.
Identifiers: LCCN 2020006294 | ISBN 9780823443482 (hardcover)
Subjects: LCSH: Walker, Kate, 1848-1931—Juvenile literature.
Women lighthouse keepers—New Jersey—Biography—Juvenile literature.
Lighthouse keepers—New Jersey—Biography—Juvenile literature. | Robbins Reef Lighthouse (N.J.)
Classification: LCC VK1140.W35 S65 2021 | DDC 387.1/55092 [B]—dc23
LC record available at https://lccn.loc.gov/2020006294

ISBN: 978-0-8234-4348-2 (hardcover)

In 1882 Kate Kaird sailed across the ocean from Germany to America with her
small son, Jacob. She was thirty-four years old, a widow, and hoped to find a better
life for them. Even though she knew only a few words of English, she quickly found
a job as a cook at the Officers' Quarters at Fort Hancock, New Jersey.

John Walker, the keeper of the Sandy Hook Lighthouse, took his meals at the Officers' Quarters. Impressed with Kate's energy and determination, he began giving her English lessons. Soon they were married.

For a year, John, Kate, and Jacob lived onshore in a large house next to the Sandy Hook Lighthouse where Kate kept a garden and a few chickens. Then John accepted a position as keeper at Robbins Reef, an offshore lighthouse in New York Bay between Manhattan and Staten Island.

Kate was unhappy about the move. She knew she would miss her friends in town, her garden, and the chickens. And where would Jacob run and play? Had she really come all the way from Germany to live in a lonely lighthouse?

From far off, Robbins Reef Lighthouse looked like a tiny candle on a birthday cake.

11

Up close, the five-story cast-iron tower loomed over their rowboat. The lighthouse stood on a granite foundation surrounded by water. Kate noticed there wasn't a blade of grass or a single flower. Except for John and Jacob, her only company would be seals and circling seagulls.

Kate followed John and Jacob up the lighthouse's steep ladder. When she reached the top, John gave her a hand onto the wide deck that wrapped around the main floor of the lighthouse. Jacob impatiently pulled his mother toward the open door.

Inside, a large circular room served as both kitchen and dining room. Lockers for clothes and cupboards for china were fitted neatly into the walls. An oilcloth was spread on the kitchen table. At the far end of the room was a large black stove for cooking that also heated the downstairs in winter.

John ushered Kate and Jacob up the winding stairs to the second-floor parlor. More steps took them to a large bedroom on the third floor, and two snug bedrooms on the fourth.

In the small watch room on the fifth floor, a door opened to a narrow catwalk with a sweeping view of Manhattan, New Jersey, Brooklyn, and Staten Island.

A steep ladder led to the topmost floor, the glassed-in lantern room. The great light stood, still and silent, in the center of the tiny room. Its polished lenses sparkled in the sunlight, bright as a diamond.

Those first few weeks Kate didn't unpack her trunks, but she hung pictures and a pendulum clock in the parlor and filled the windowsills with flowerpots and plants. She put down bright scatter rugs in all the rooms. In the kitchen, she settled her rocking chair next to the big black stove and moved her sewing machine under one of the windows where the light was good.

Slowly, Robbins Reef began to feel more like a home, *her* home. And Kate decided to unpack.

Once or twice a week, if the weather was good, John or Kate rowed to Staten Island for fresh food, supplies, newspapers, and the mail. Sometimes Kate visited with friends she'd made there before rowing back to the lighthouse. Jacob boarded with a family in town and went to school, but he spent his weekends and summers at Robbins Reef.

Kate applied to the United States Lighthouse Board for the job of assistant keeper. John had taught her a lot about keeping a lighthouse when they lived at Sandy Hook. Soon a letter arrived with good news. Kate had got the job!

The work at Robbins Reef filled their days and nights. In the keeper's daily log, a new day started at twelve noon, not midnight. John and Kate had to record exactly how much coal and kerosene they used each day. They noted the wind and weather. If a ship foundered on the reef, or a fisherman needed to be rescued, that went in the logbook too.

They polished the brass work on the light every day and cleaned the lenses once a month, a two-day job. Each morning they filled five-gallon cans with kerosene so that all was ready for the night watch.

At sunset, regular as clockwork, gunfire and a bugle call at Fort Jay on nearby Governors Island signaled it was time to light the lamp. All through the night, John and Kate took turns keeping watch, refilling the lamp when the kerosene was low, trimming the wicks so they wouldn't smoke, and rewinding the pulley mechanism that kept the light flashing.

On foggy nights when the lighthouse beacon could not be seen, no one got any sleep. They had to fire up the steam engine in the basement that sent siren blasts every three seconds to warn passing ships about the dangerous shoals next to the lighthouse. If the steam engine broke down, one of them hammered on a bell on the catwalk outside the watch room until the fog lifted.

Their first spring at Robbins Reef, Kate and John's daughter, Mae, was born. In October the Statue of Liberty opened. They watched the celebration through binoculars from the catwalk. There were bands, speeches, and fireworks.

Several happy years passed. In the evenings after supper, Kate's sewing machine hummed. Little Mae played with her toys and dolls. John might page through a week's packet of newspapers before beginning the night watch. Or one of them would choose a book to read from the traveling library that circulated from lighthouse to lighthouse.

Sometimes late in the evening Robbins Reef felt like a ship peacefully at anchor. Life in a lighthouse had its rhythms, Kate thought, as the soft sound of lapping water lulled her gently to sleep.

Then one bitter February when Mae was three, John came down with pneumonia. Day and night, Kate nursed him, all the while tending the light and looking after Mae.

John needed to see a doctor, but the harbor was choked with ice and a trip to Staten Island would be dangerous. When he did not get better, Kate raised the distress signal—the American flag flown upside down—and prayed that help would come.

Soon men from the Lighthouse Depot on Staten Island came to take John to the hospital.

Bundled in blankets, John looked up at Kate as he was helped into their small boat and said, "Mind the light, Kate."

Kate squeezed his hand. Of course she must stay behind and mind the light! The passing ships depended on it, and lives would be lost if the light went dark.

Days went by without any word. Finally Kate spied a small boat rowing slowly out to the lighthouse. The oarsman was alone. Kate knew the news was bad. John had died.

A letter came from the Lighthouse Board informing Kate she must leave Robbins Reef in ten days. But Kate persuaded the board to let her stay on until a replacement could be found. For four years Kate worked as temporary keeper at low pay while the Lighthouse Board searched for a man to do the job. Two men turned down the post because they said it would be too lonely.

Finally, in 1895, Kate was hired as permanent keeper and got a raise, making her one of the first women on the Eastern Seaboard to be put in charge of an offshore lighthouse. A year later, Jacob, now twenty, was hired as her assistant. Jacob lived part of the time on Staten Island where he was courting his sweetheart, Loretta, and where Mae was going to school. But several times a week he rowed to the lighthouse with supplies and took the night watch.

28

There were no days off for Kate, not even on holidays.

One Christmas, Kate encouraged Jacob and Mae to spend the day on Staten Island with friends. All day she kept an eye on the weather. A light snow began to fall. Then it grew heavier and changed to sleet. Kate knew her children would not try to row back to the lighthouse that night.

As darkness fell, Kate started the siren. The wind picked up and Kate heard a frightening sound out on the deck. One of the chains holding the lighthouse dory had come loose. She would have to go out and reattach the rowboat or lose her only lifeline to the outside world.

Kate opened the door and stepped onto the icy deck. The wind nearly whirled her off the landing. As she neared the dory, the loose chain hit her in the eye. Finally, her frozen fingers secured the boat. Then Kate crawled back to the lighthouse door. Once inside, she sat down to a simple supper and counted her blessings.

Although life at Robbins Reef could be lonely and hard in the winter, when summer came Kate's friends from Staten Island would row out to the lighthouse for picnics.

During one visit, Kate and her friends were sitting outside on the open deck, drinking tea and enjoying the afternoon. Watching the constantly changing waterfront traffic was better than any parade. One of her friends asked her if she was ever lonely.

"Lonely?" said Kate. "Of course. But there are worse things than loneliness. Loneliness has taught me I can be a fairly entertaining companion for myself. . . . And there are advantages. No burglars, no prying neighbors, no gossip, and plenty of fresh air!"

Kate became known for her rescues. One took place on a stormy winter day. Kate and Jacob watched through binoculars as a schooner foundered on the reef, then rolled over on its side.

Jacob wanted to go, but Kate insisted that she would.

She threw on her oilskin and sou'wester and lowered the lighthouse dory into the churning black water. The wind cut into her like a knife as she rowed toward the struggling crew.

When she reached the men, she helped them, one by one, into the boat. After the five were safely aboard, the captain looked around for his dog, Scotty. That's when Kate saw a small, exhausted terrier paddling in the waves.

Kate maneuvered the boat close to Scotty and fished him out of the water with an oar. The poor dog lay at her feet, cold and limp.

For two hours Kate and the men took turns rowing against the wind and strong currents.

When they got back to the lighthouse, Kate wrapped Scotty in a blanket and put him on the rug next to the stove. In bad weather, Kate always kept a pot of hot coffee on the stove. She poured a cup, black as tar, down Scotty's throat. The dog's eyes opened in surprise, then he gasped and shivered.

After the storm died down, Jacob rowed the rescued men to the mainland. The captain promised to be back in a few days for Scotty. By the time he returned, Kate and Scotty had become good friends. As the captain and Scotty were leaving, the dog gave Kate a look of gratitude she would never forget.

One day a letter came from the Lighthouse Board saying it was time for Kate to retire. The new retirement age was seventy, and Kate was seventy-one. She had lived at Robbins Reef for thirty-three years and rescued more than fifty people.

Kate moved to a cottage on Staten Island with Mae, where she could be near her family and friends. Reporters from as far away as California and Canada came to write stories about Kate. Her eyes lit up or filled with tears as she recalled happy times and sad.

"Every morning when the sun came up," she remembered, "I stood at the window and looked toward John's grave. Sometimes the hills were brown, and sometimes green, and sometimes white with snow. But they always brought the same message, something I heard him say more often than anything else. Just three words: *Mind the light*."

About Kate Walker

Kate's Light is based on a true story. Katherine Gortler was born in Germany in 1848 and grew up there. As a young woman, she married Joseph Kaird and had a son, Jacob. Soon after, her husband died, so Kate decided to emigrate to America where there were more opportunities. It was a brave decision for someone who did not speak a word of English.

After Kate married John Walker and moved to Robbins Reef in 1885, she had to adapt to the challenges of living in an offshore lighthouse. At the time, Robbins Reef was one of the most up-to-date lighthouses on the East Coast. The original granite lighthouse from 1839 had been replaced in 1883 with one made of cast iron. Equipped with a powerful fourth-order Fresnel lens, its flashing beacon could be seen on a clear night from as far away as seven nautical miles. But Kate lived without the conveniences of modern life. The rooms were lit with kerosene lamps. Because the lighthouse had no electricity, Kate had no refrigerator, washing

machine, or electric iron, and no hot water except for what she could heat on the coal stove in the kitchen. A cistern in the basement held filtered rainwater that was pumped by hand to the first floor. There was no indoor plumbing. With no central heating, the upper floors of the lighthouse were cold in winter.

And, of course, there were no telephones or cell phones, no radio or television, no movies, and no Internet or e-mail. Communication was either in person or by handwritten letters that could take days or even weeks to reach their destination. For entertainment, the Walkers had a gramophone and a traveling library, a chest of books supplied by the Lighthouse Board that was replaced every few months with new titles.

Visits by the lighthouse tender, a supply ship that visited lighthouses up and down the coast, were rare. Once a year, the tender came by with supplies meant to last for the next twelve months and winched them onto the deck with a crane: six tons of coal for the stove poured down the lighthouse's coal chute into the basement, and barrels of kerosene were transferred from the tender to the deck. The tender also brought Kate's wages for the year—$350 when she was John's assistant and $600 when she was finally promoted to lightkeeper in 1895. Occasionally there were inspections, which Kate always passed with flying colors.

For trips to Staten Island, Kate used the lighthouse dory, a rowboat fitted with oars but no motor. An expert rower like Kate might make the mile-long trip in a half hour in good weather, or two or three hours if the waves were rough. Sometimes, especially in the winter when the weather was bad, it was not safe to go at all. Although Kate was entitled to days off each month (the Lighthouse Depot, a central office and warehouse on Staten Island, would have sent out a substitute to fill in for Kate), she seldom left the lighthouse for more than seven or eight hours at a time, and always with an eye on the weather since storms could come up unexpectedly.

Six years after John Walker's death, Jacob was appointed assistant keeper of Robbins Reef. He divided his time between Robbins Reef and Staten Island where he lived with his wife, Loretta, and their children. (For several years before his children were school age, Jacob and his family lived with Kate at Robbins Reef.) After Kate retired in 1919, Jacob was promoted and stayed on for two years as keeper of the lighthouse.

Kate died in 1931, but she is not forgotten. Even now sailors sometimes refer to Robbins Reef as "Kate's Light." In 1996, the Coast Guard honored Kate by naming one of its cutters the USCGC *Katherine Walker*. Two years later, the United States Postal Service celebrated Kate's one hundred fiftieth birthday by issuing a special commemorative envelope with her picture on it.

The last keeper left Robbins Reef in 1966, when the light was automated by the Coast Guard. For many years after that, the lighthouse stood empty and neglected. Now it is being restored by the Noble Maritime Collection on Staten Island. Some day,

visitors will be able to see the lighthouse just as it was when Kate lived there. They will be able to stand on the catwalk where Kate stood for thirty-three years, binoculars in hand, looking out to busy New York Harbor, faithfully minding the light.

Notes

Endpaper image courtesy of the Library of Congress reproduction number: LC-DIG-pga-00863

Photographs on pgs. 35, 36 courtesy of the Noble Maritime Collection.

Pg. 26   *"Mind the light, Kate."*: Urban, Erin M. *Perspective: Robbins Reef.* Staten Island, New York: The Noble Maritime Collection, 2016: pg. 24.

Pg. 30   *"Lonely?"*: Bird, Carol. "The Loneliest Woman in the World." *Philadelphia Public Ledger,* August 25, 1925.

Pg. 34   *"Every morning when the sun came up,"*: Urban, Erin M. *Perspective: Robbins Reef.* Staten Island, New York: The Noble Maritime Collection, 2016: pg. 24.

Additional Sources

Clifford, Mary Louise, and J. Candace, Clifford. *Women Who Kept the Lights: An Illustrated History of Female Lighthouse Keepers.* (Alexandria, Virginia: Cypress Communications, 2001), pgs. 166–175.

Harrison, Timothy E. "Kate Would Be Proud." *Lighthouse Digest,* March/April 2011: pgs. 40–45.

Hemmingway, William. "The Woman of the Light." *Harper's Weekly,* August 14, 1909: pgs. 11–12.

"Kept House Nineteen Years on Robbins Reef." *New York Times,* March 5, 1905: Section 3: pg. 7.

"Mrs. Walker Dies; Lighthouse Keeper." *New York Times,* February 7, 1931: pg. 12.

For further information, see lighthousefriends.com/light.asp?ID=582.

To learn more about Kate Walker, the history of Robbins Reef Lighthouse, and the restoration efforts, please visit www.noblemaritime.org/robbins-reef.

BROOKLYN

GOVERNORS ISLAND

MANHATTAN